RAND McNALLY®

Junior Classroom Atlas

4th Edition

Cartography
Gregory Babiak
Rob Ferry

Design Director
Joerg Metzner

Graphic Designer
Jennifer Stewart

Photo Credits
l = left, c = center, r = right, t = top, b = bottom
Cover: all ©istockphoto; p. 4 ©Lostutnikov/Shutterstock; p. 5 ©istockphoto; p. 7 ©istockphoto; p. 9 ©istockphoto; p. 10 t ©istockphoto, tc ©istockphoto, bc ©Jess Kraft/Shutterstock, b ©istockphoto; p. 11 ©istockphoto; p. 12 t ©Joyce Sherwin/Shutterstock, tc ©istockphoto, bc ©istockphoto, b ©istockphoto; p. 13 all ©istockphoto; p. 14 ©istockphoto; p. 16-17 all ©istockphoto; p. 18 ©istockphoto; p. 19 (timeline l to r) ©istockphoto, ©Everett Historical/Shutterstock, ©istockphoto, ©istockphoto, ©istockphoto; tl ©Tao Jiang/Shutterstock, tc ©istockphoto, tr ©istockphoto, cl ©istockphoto, c ©age fotostock/Alamy, cr ©istockphoto; p. 20 ©istockphoto; p. 21 (timeline l to r) ©Anton_Ivanov/Shutterstock, ©istockphoto, ©istockphoto, ©Hola Images/Alamy, ©istockphoto; tl ©Trent Townsend/Shutterstock, tr ©istockphoto, cl ©Fred Cardoso/Shutterstock, c ©Anton_Ivanov/Shutterstock, cr ©istockphoto; p. 23 ©istockphoto; p. 24-25 (timeline l to r) ©Tanjala Gica/Shutterstock, ©Nick Pavlakis/Shutterstock, ©mountainpix/Shutterstock, ©JeniFoto/Shutterstock, ©ndphoto/Shutterstock, ©Everett Historical/Shutterstock, ©BMCL/Shutterstock, ©timsimages/Shutterstock; p. 24 tl ©barbar34/Shutterstock, tr ©beboy/Shutterstock, cl ©Fedor Selivanov/Shutterstock, cr ©S. Borisov/Shutterstock; p. 25 tl ©Lenar Musin/Shutterstock, tr ©istockphoto, cl ©istockphoto, c ©Mikhailo/Shutterstock, cr ©mRGB/Shutterstock; p. 26 ©istockphoto; p. 27 (timeline l to r) ©istockphoto, ©istockphoto, ©Anders Blomqvist/Lonely Planet Images, ©Milana Tkachenko/Shutterstock, ©istockphoto, ©yui/Shutterstock; tl ©istockphoto, cl ©istockphoto, c ©istockphoto, cl ©istockphoto; p. 29 ©istockphoto; p 30-31 (timeline all) ©istockphoto; p. 30 tl ©istockphoto, tc ©istockphoto, tr ©istockphoto, cl ©Everything/Shutterstock, c ©istockphoto, cr ©istockphoto; p. 31 all ©istockphoto; p. 32 ©istockphoto; p. 33 (timeline l to r) ©Sasapee/Shutterstock, ©f9photos/Shutterstock, ©istockphoto, ©istockphoto, ©istockphoto; tl ©Natalia Fadosova/Shutterstock, tr ©istockphoto, cl ©Stanilav Fosenbauer/Shutterstock, c ©Jason Ho/Shutterstock, cr ©Brian Kinney/Shutterstock; p. 34 ©istockphoto; p. 35 (timeline l to r) ©Denis Burdin/Shutterstock, ©f9photos/Shutterstock, ©I. Noyan Yilmaz/Shutterstock; tc ©istockphoto, tr ©Anton_Ivanov/Shutterstock, cl ©Footage.Pro/Shutterstock, c ©Matt Berger/Shutterstock, cr ©Jan Martin Will/Shutterstock; p. 36 all ©istockphoto; p. 37 all ©istockphoto; p. 38 ©istockphoto; p. 39 all ©istockphoto; p. 41 ©istockphoto; p. 43 ©istockphoto.

Published and printed in U.S.A.
August 2024
PO# 78841
ISBN: 0-528-02692-5
ISBN-13: 978-0-528-02692-8

If you have a comment, suggestion, or even a compliment, please contact us at
printproducts@randmcnally.com.

randpublishing.com

RAND McNALLY PUBLISHING

Table of Contents

Maps and Globes

Maps and globes help people learn about the earth.
A **globe** is a model of the earth.
A **map** is a drawing of the earth's surface.

Earth from space

The earth is shaped like a **sphere**, or ball. This picture taken from space shows some of the earth's land and water through clouds.

Did You Know?

Water covers about three-fourths of the earth's surface. From space the earth looks blue.

A globe is shaped like the earth. When you turn the globe, you see a different part of the earth.

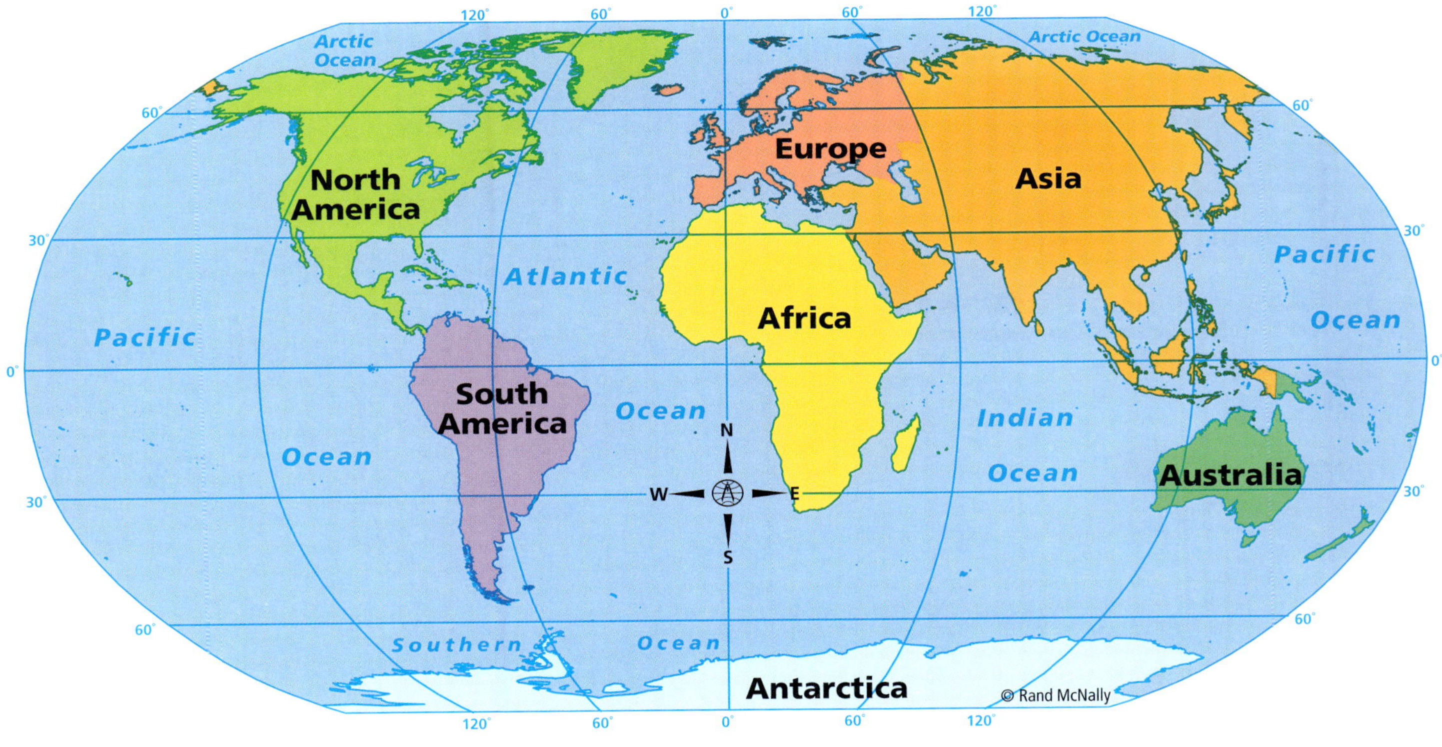

A map is flat. It can show all of the earth's surface at once.

Map Question
How is a map different from a globe?

The World's Land and Water

The world is made up of land and water. **Continents** are the largest bodies of land. **Oceans** are the largest bodies of water.

Map Question

Which ocean is between the continents of North America and Europe?

The World's Countries

The world's continents are divided into **countries**.
A **country boundary** shows where a country begins and ends.

Map Question

Trace the country boundaries of the United States.

What countries does the United States touch?

World Land Use

People use the world's land in different ways. Many people in cities earn a living by **manufacturing**, or making goods.

Forestry in North America

Trees from North America's forests provide such things as lumber for building houses and pulp for making paper.

Trade in Europe

Europe has many busy ports where ships load and unload goods from around the world.

Herding in South America

Herders in some parts of South America raise llamas. These animals provide wool and transportation.

Farming in Asia

Rice is the most important crop grown in Asia. It can be grown on flat land or even on steep hillsides.

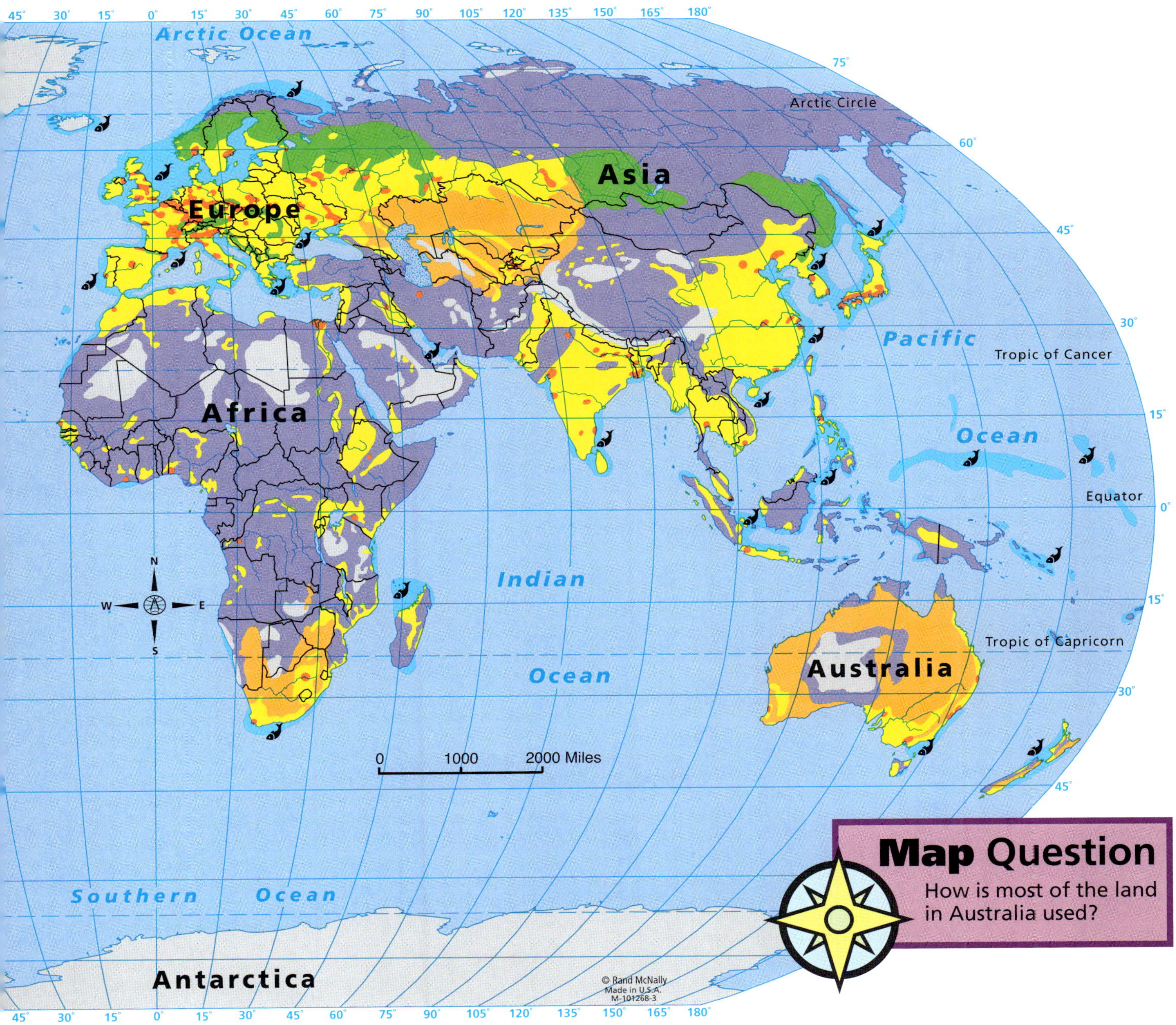

Map Question

How is most of the land in Australia used?

World Climate

Climate is how hot or cold, wet or dry a place is.
Some places have a climate that changes with the seasons.

Cross-country skiing in Canada
Parts of Canada have long, cold winters and short, cool summers.

Rain forest in Brazil
Rain forests receive more than 80 inches of rain a year. Many of the world's rain forests are near the equator.

Olive groves in Spain
Parts of Spain have hot, dry summers and rainy winters.

Farming in Indonesia
Rice grows well in places that are hot and rainy all year.

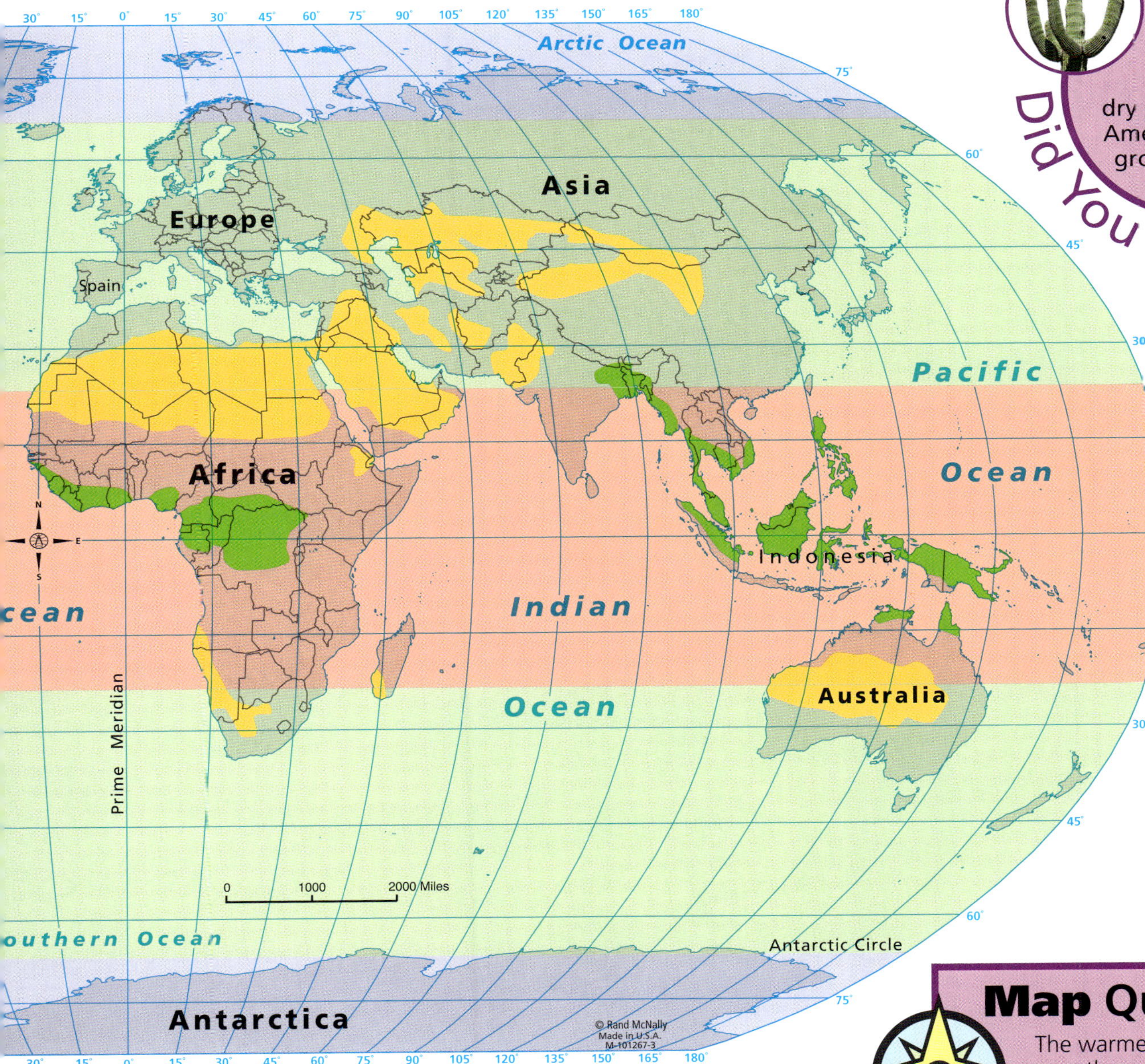

Did You Know?

A saguaro is a giant cactus that grows in very dry places in North America. It may grow to be 60 feet tall.

Map Question

The warmest climates are near the equator.

Where are the coldest climates?

Average Yearly Rainfall

Deserts are the world's driest places. Rain forests are the wettest places.

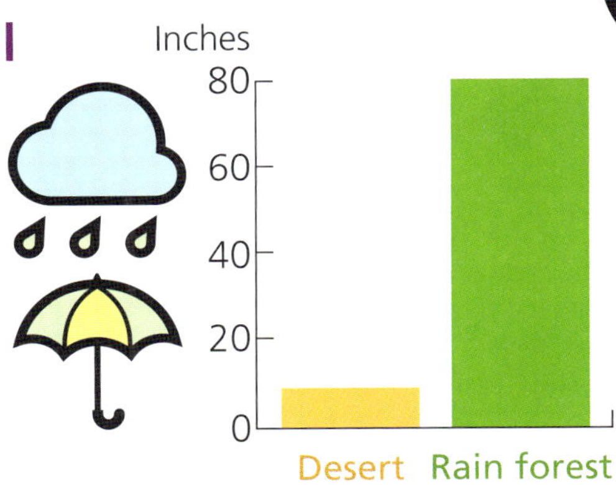

United States

The **United States** is made up of fifty states.
Each state has a **state capital**, which is a city where state government leaders work.

Map Question
What city is the capital of your state?

United States
Country boundary
State boundary
River
Canada
Country
Ohio
State
Washington, D.C.
Country capital
Denver
State capital
Dallas
City
Atlantic Ocean
Ocean
Swamp
Great Lakes
Lake Superior
Lake Michigan
Lake Huron
Lake Erie
Lake Ontario
Minnesota
Wisconsin
Michigan
Iowa
Illinois
Indiana
Ohio
Pennsylvania
New York
Vermont
New Hampshire
Maine
Mass.
Conn.
R.I.
New Jersey
Delaware
Maryland
West Virginia
Virginia
Kentucky
Missouri
Arkansas
Tennessee
North Carolina
South Carolina
Georgia
Alabama
Mississippi
Louisiana
Florida
Appalachian Mountains
Mississippi River
Missouri River
Ohio River
Illinois River
Tennessee River
Trinity River
Gulf of Mexico
Atlantic Ocean
Bahamas
Cape Cod
Long Island
Cape Hatteras
Cape Canaveral
The Everglades
Florida Keys
St. Paul
Minneapolis
Green Bay
Milwaukee
Madison
Rockford
Chicago
Peoria
Springfield
Grand Rapids
Lansing
Detroit
Cleveland
Columbus
Cincinnati
Indianapolis
Evansville
Louisville
Frankfort
Pittsburgh
Harrisburg
Philadelphia
Trenton
New York
Buffalo
Albany
Montpelier
Concord
Augusta
Portland
Boston
Providence
Hartford
Dover
Baltimore
Annapolis
Washington, D.C.
Charleston
Richmond
Norfolk
Winston-Salem
Raleigh
Charlotte
Columbia
Charleston
Nashville
Memphis
Atlanta
Columbus
Birmingham
Montgomery
Jackson
Baton Rouge
New Orleans
Tallahassee
Jacksonville
Orlando
Tampa
Miami
Sioux City
Cedar Rapids
Des Moines
Kansas City
St. Louis
Jefferson City
Tulsa
Fort Smith
Little Rock
Shreveport
Houston
N
S
E
W
0
100
200
300
400 Miles
95°
90°
85°
80°
75°
70°
65°
45°
40°
35°
©Rand McNally
Made in U.S.A.
M-101131-1

United States Regions

The United States can be divided into regions in many different ways. This map shows one way.

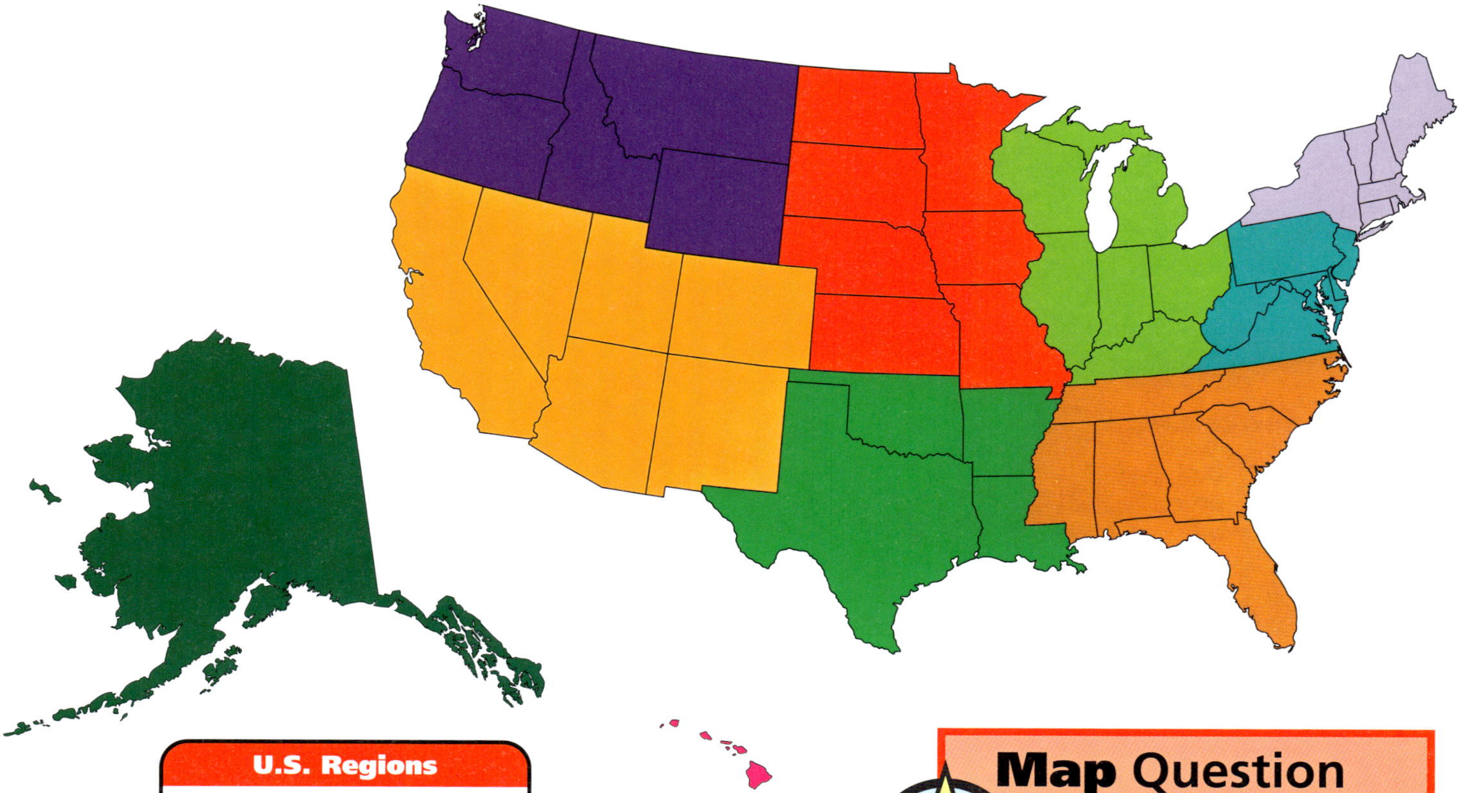

U.S. Regions

- Northeast Region
- Mid-Atlantic Region
- Southeast Region
- Midwest Region
- North Central Region
- South Central Region
- Southwest Region
- Northwest Region
- Alaska
- Hawaii

Map Question

The color frames around the photos match the colors of the regions on the map.

In which region is the national capital located?

The United States through History

About 1,200 years ago
The Hohokam farmed in the desert Southwest.

About 1,000 years ago
Vikings from Greenland explored the northeast coast of North America.

About 800 years ago
The Anasazi built cliff dwellings in the Southwest.

900 A.D — 1000 A.D. — 1100 — 1200 — 1300 — 1400

Fall in Maine

The United States Capitol building in Washington, D.C.

Did You Know?

Washington, D.C., is not part of any state. It occupies a federal district called the District of Columbia.

The Outer Banks of North Carolina

Farms in Wisconsin

Badlands of South Dakota

A bayou in Louisiana

The Grand Canyon in Arizona

Seattle, Washington

About 500 years ago
Spanish explorers traveled through the south and southwestern parts of what is now the United States.

About 400 years ago
English settlers started colonies along the Atlantic Coast.

A little more than 200 years ago
The colonies won freedom from Great Britain, and the United States became a nation.

About 100 years ago
Millions of European immigrants settled in the United States.

1500 — 1600 — 1700 — 1800 — 1900 — 2000

North America

North America is the continent where we live. The United States is the second-largest country in North America.

Map Question

North America's largest country is a little larger than the United States.

What country is it?

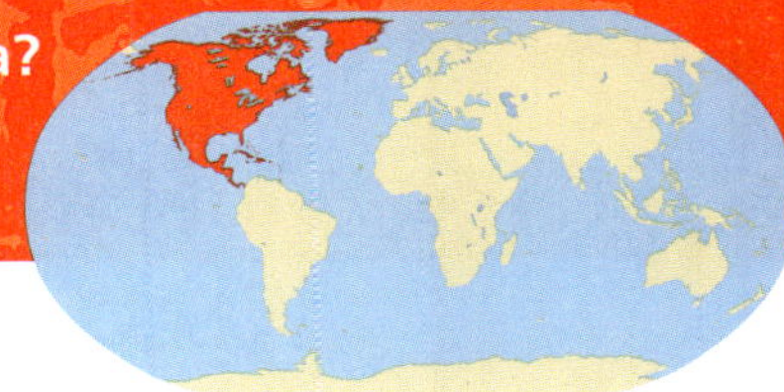

Comparing Countries in North America

The United States and Canada are almost the same size. The United States has more people than any other country in North America.

Grizzly bears are found mostly in Alaska and western Canada.

Did You Know?

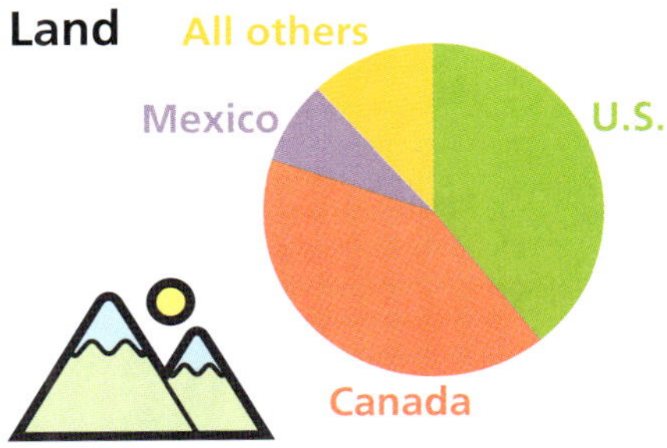

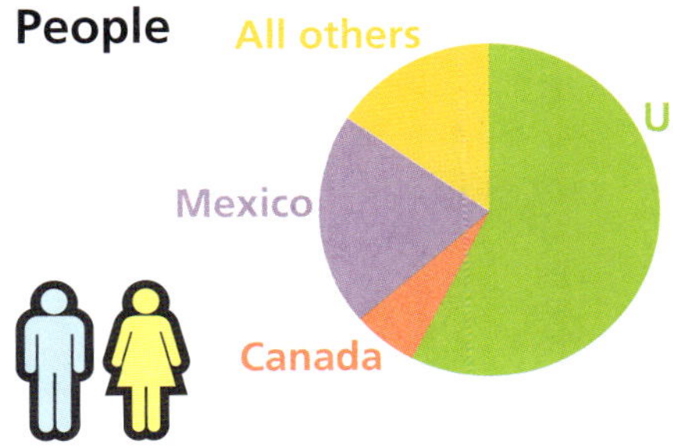

Wheat field on the Great Plains
The Great Plains region stretches through Canada and the United States. Wheat is the major crop.

National University in Mexico City
Mexico City is a center of art and learning. This school is the largest university in Mexico.

The Statue of Liberty in New York Harbor
The Statue of Liberty welcomes people from other countries who come to live in the United States.

North America through History

About 700 years ago
The Aztecs built an empire in Mexico.

About 500 years ago
Europeans explored North America.

About 400 years ago
Europeans started colonies in North America.

About 200 years ago
The United States became a nation.

About 100 years ago
The Panama Canal linked the Atlantic and Pacific Oceans.

1300 — 1400 — 1500 — 1600 — 1700 — 1800 — 1900 — 2000

South America

South America has thirteen mainland countries. All but two of them are located along a coast.

Map Question

Which two South American countries are not along a coast?

Where in the world is South America?

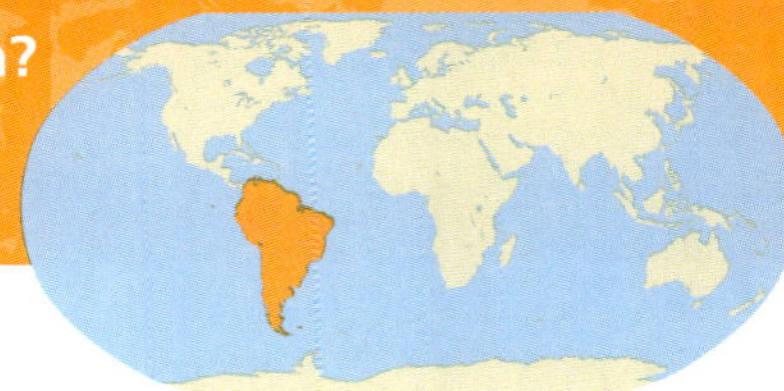

Did You Know? The giant tortoises of the Galapagos Islands can live for more than 140 years.

That's a Lot of Coffee!

Brazil and Colombia produce more coffee beans than any other countries in the world.

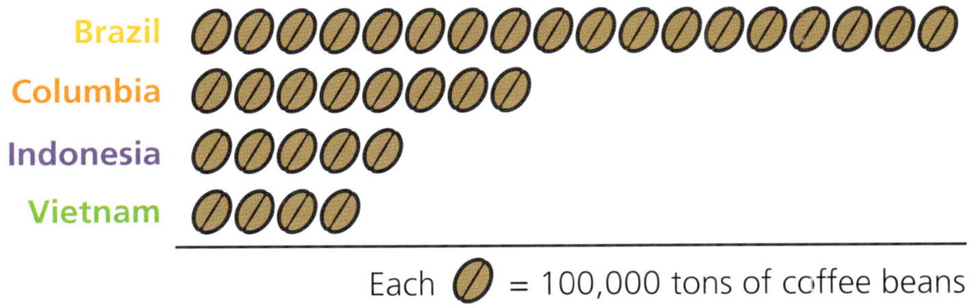

Amazon rain forest in Brazil

The world's largest tropical rain forest covers most of northern South America.

Machu Picchu in Peru

The stone ruins of this ancient Inca city are high in the Andes Mountains.

Outdoor market in Bolivia

Indians from villages in the Andes gather to buy and sell goods.

South America through History

About 600 years ago The Inca ruled lands along the west coast of South America.

About 400 years ago Spain ruled much of South America.

About 100 years ago One million people lived in Buenos Aires, Argentina.

1400 — 1500 — 1600 — 1700 — 1800 — 1900 — 2000

About 500 years ago Portugal claimed Brazil.

About 200 years ago South American countries won their freedom from European rulers.

Europe

Europe is a small continent, but it has many people. It has some of the world's most famous cities.

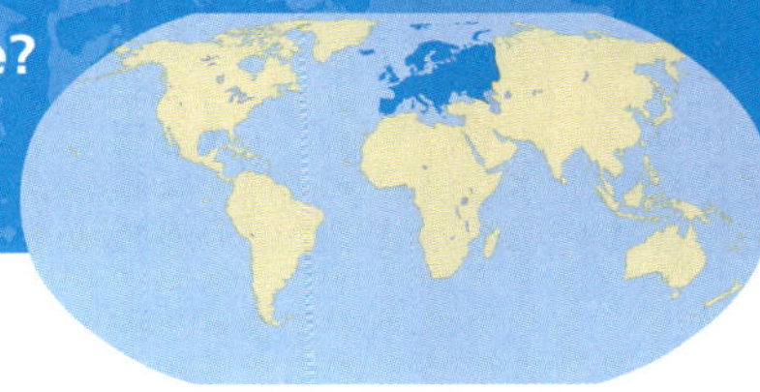

Map Question

Moscow is Europe's largest city.

In what country is it located?

Europe

The Parthenon in Athens, Greece

This ancient temple was built by the Greeks to honor the goddess Athena.

The Eiffel Tower in Paris, France

The Eiffel Tower is a popular place for tourists to visit. They can go to the top of the 984-foot tower for a view of Paris.

The Colosseum in Rome, Italy

This large outdoor amphitheater was built by the Romans almost 2,000 years ago.

Tower of Big Ben in London, England

Big Ben is a famous bell in the clock tower of the Houses of Parliament in London.

Europe through History

About 5,000 years ago
Minoan culture began on the island of Crete.

About 4,500 years ago
Greek civilization began.

About 2,000 years ago
The Roman Empire ruled a huge area around the Mediterranean Sea.

About 1,000 years ago
Towns began to grow in Europe.

About 700 years ago
The Renaissance brought new interest in art and science.

3000 B.C. — 2000 B.C. — 1000 B.C. — 1000 A.D. — 1100 — 1200 — 1300

Did You Know?

The Matterhorn is one of the most famous mountains in the world.

How many people?

This graph compares the populations of five of Europe's largest cities.

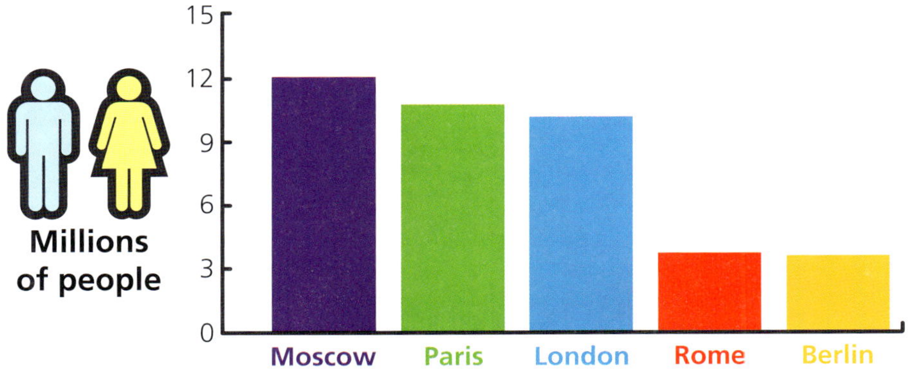

Basketmaker in Scotland

Europe has many factories, but some workers make goods by hand.

High-speed train in France

Express trains carry passengers to major cities throughout Europe.

Skiing in the Alps

Winter sports are popular in many parts of Europe.

1400 | 1500 | 1600 | 1700 | 1800 | 1900 | 2000

About 500 years ago
Europeans began to explore the world.

About 300 years ago
The Industrial Revolution brought many new ways of making goods.

About 200 years ago
European nations set up colonies in Africa and Asia.

About 70 years ago
Many European cities were destroyed in World War II.

Africa

Africa has both rain forests and deserts. The Sahara is the largest desert in the world. It covers most of the northern part of the continent.

Map Question

What desert is found along the Atlantic coast in the southern part of Africa?

Where in the world is Africa?

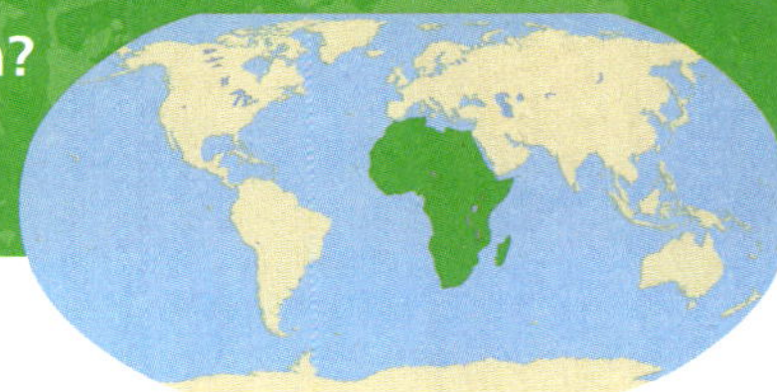

Did You Know?

The Great Sphinx in Egypt is a huge statue with the head of a man and the body of a lion.

The Longest River on Each Continent

The Nile River in Africa is the longest river in the world.

- **Nile** (Africa) — 4,145 miles
- **Amazon** (South America) — 4,000 miles
- **Yangtze** (Asia) — 3,900 miles
- **Mississippi-Missouri** (North America) — 3,740 miles
- **Murray-Darling** (Australia) — 2,330 miles
- **Volga** (Europe) — 2,194 miles

Ancient statues in Egypt

These giant statues were carved thousands of years ago. They were part of a temple honoring an Egyptian king.

Lowland gorillas in central Africa

Lowland gorillas live in rain forests near the equator.

Modern buildings in Johannesburg, South Africa

Johannesburg is the largest city in South Africa. It is one of Africa's most important trade centers.

Africa through History

About 5,100 years ago
Egypt became a great kingdom.

3000 B.C.

About 4,000 years ago
The kingdom of Kush became a center of art, learning, and trade.

1000 B.C.

About 600 years ago
Powerful kingdoms began in central and southern Africa.

1400 A.D.

About 500 years ago
Portuguese explorers sailed around Africa to India.

1600

1800

About 100 years ago
European countries ruled most of Africa.

About 60 years ago
African countries began to win freedom from European rule.

2000

Asia

Asia is the largest continent. It has more land and more people than any other continent.

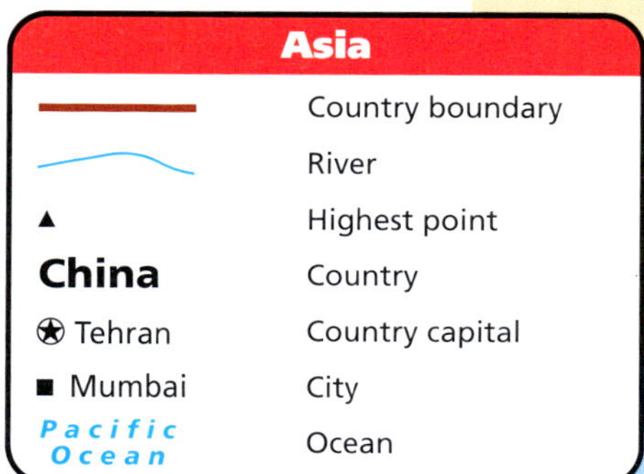

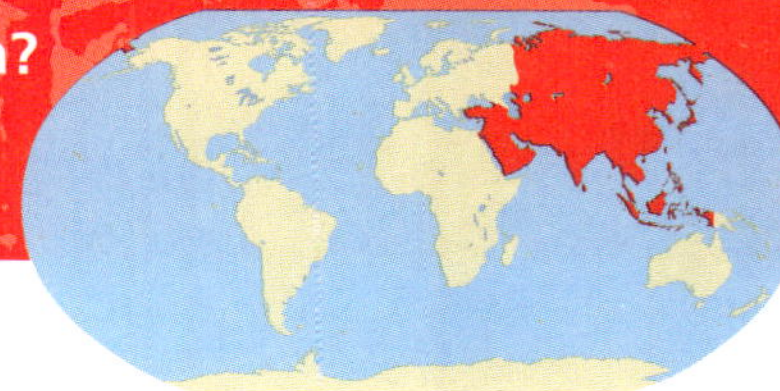

Eurasia

The continents of Europe and Asia form one large body of land called Eurasia.

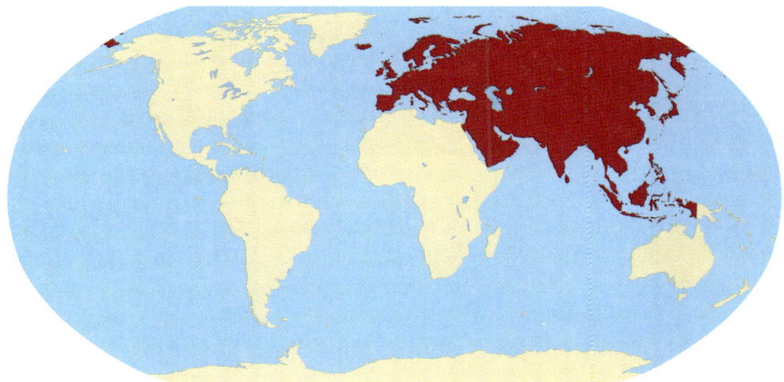

Map Question

The world's largest country covers much of Asia and Europe.

What country is it?

Asia

Farming in India
Some farmers in Asia use animals to pull plows.

Transportation in China
Many people use bicycles to get around in China's crowded cities.

Oil refinery in Southwest Asia
Much of the world's oil comes from countries in Southwest Asia.

Hong Kong Harbor
Hong Kong is one of the most important port cities in Asia.

The Himalayas in Nepal
The Himalayas are the highest mountains in the world. Their name means "House of Snow."

Ancient ruins in Turkey
Turkey is the westernmost country in Asia.

Asia through History

About 11,000 years ago
People began farming in Southwest Asia.

9000 B.C.

7000 B.C.

5000 B.C.

About 5,500 years ago
Civilization began between the Tigris and Euphrates Rivers.

3000 B.C.

About 2,200 years ago
China began building the Great Wall.

1000 B.C.

About 1,900 years ago
The Chinese invented paper.

1000 A.D.

Did You Know?

Giant pandas live in China's bamboo forests. They weigh up to 350 pounds.

World Population

Asia has more people than all the other continents added together.

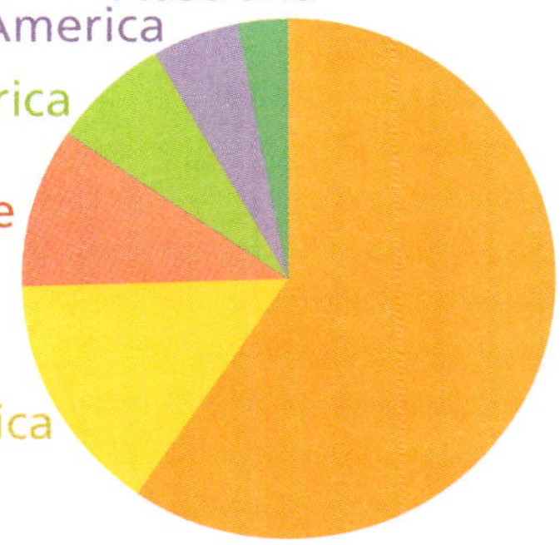

The Taj Mahal in India

An Indian ruler built the Taj Mahal in memory of h s wife. The beautiful building is made of white marble.

Skyscrapers in Tokyo, Japan

Tokyo is the capital of Japan. It is the largest city in the world.

The Great Wall of China

The Chinese built the Great Wall to protect their country. It is about 25 feet high and 4,600 miles long.

1200 — 1400 — 1600 — 1800 — 2000

About 400 years ago
The Taj Mahal was built in India.

About 200 years ago
European nations controlled parts of Asia.

About 60 years ago
India and other Asian nations won freedom.

Australia

Australia is both a continent and a country. It is the world's smallest continent, but it is the sixth-largest country.

Australia

(blue line)	River
▲	Highest point
Australia	Country
⍟ Canberra	Country capital
■ Melbourne	City
Pacific Ocean	Ocean

Map Question

What is the only country capital on the continent of Australia?

Did You Know?

A kangaroo can hop as fast as 30 miles per hour. It can jump six feet high.

Leading Sheep-Raising Countries

Australia is the world's leading producer of sheep and wool.

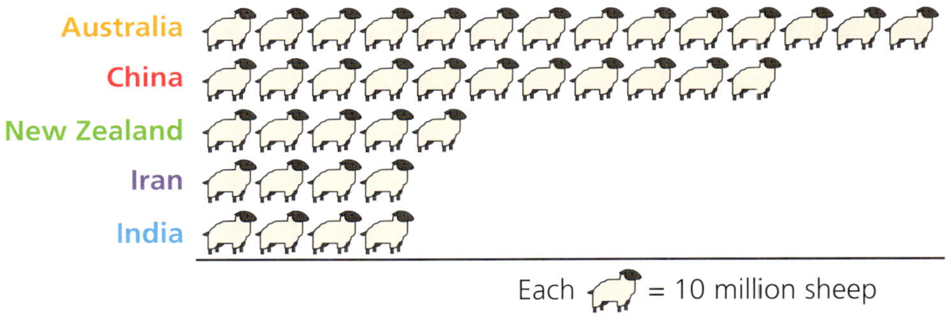

Uluru, near Alice Springs

Uluru is also called Ayers Rock. It has many caves with paintings made by people who lived there long ago.

Sydney Opera House and skyline

Sydney is the largest city in Australia. The Sydney Opera House is the city's most famous landmark.

The Great Barrier Reef

Divers can see many kinds of fish and coral along the Great Barrier Reef. The reef stretches for more than 1,200 miles along the northeast coast of Australia.

Australia through History

1400 – 1500 – 1600 – 1700 – 1800 – 1900 – 2000

About 600 years ago
Chinese settlers arrived in northern Australia.

About 400 years ago
Dutch sailors explored the coasts of Australia.

About 200 years ago
Great Britain began to claim land in Australia.

About 150 years ago
Gold was discovered in Australia.

About 100 years ago
Australia became a nation.

Antarctica

Antarctica is the coldest continent. A thick layer of ice and snow covers most of the land.

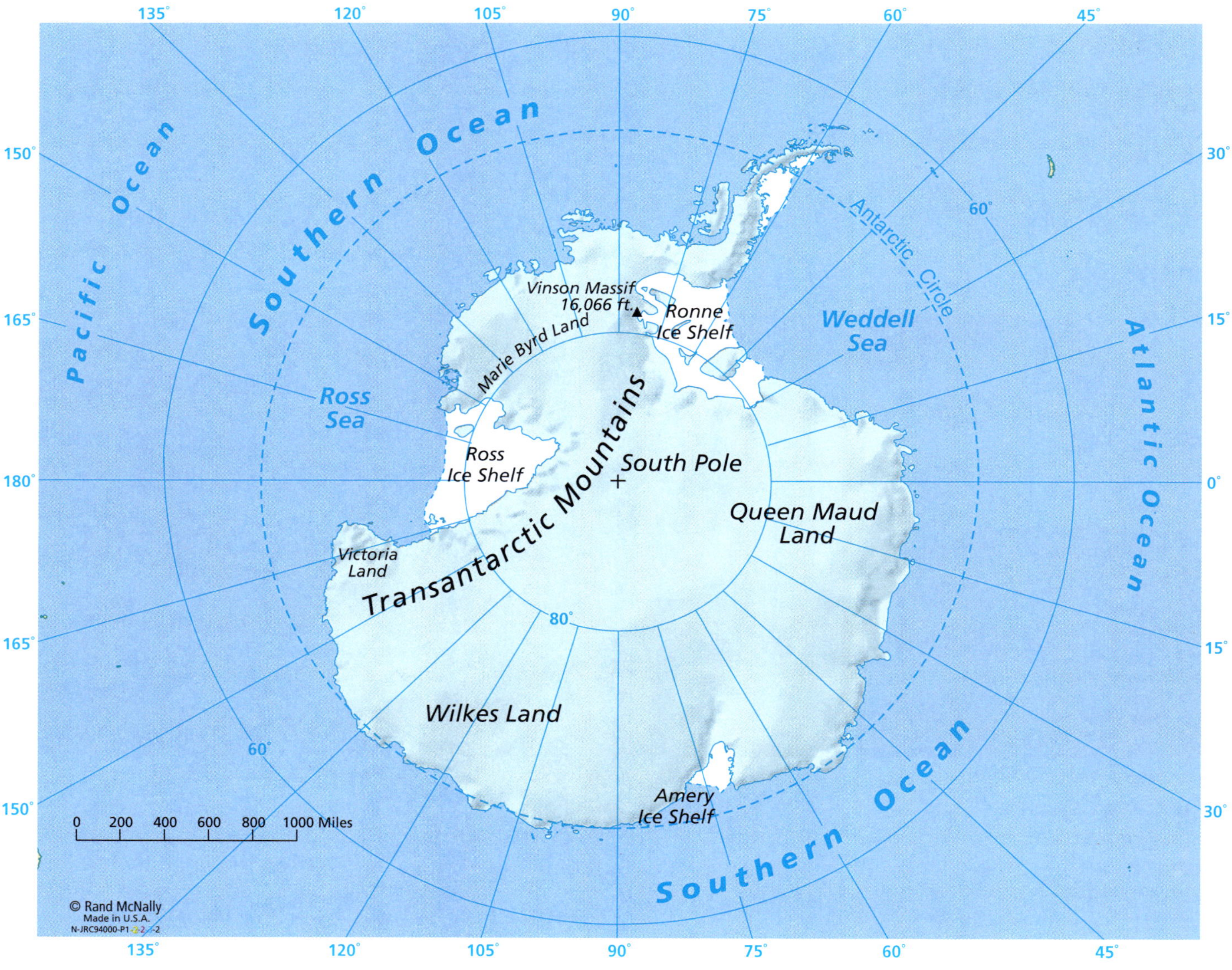

Map Question

What is the highest point in Antarctica?

Antarctica

▲	Highest point
□	Ice shelf
Pacific Ocean	Ocean

Where in the world is Antarctica?

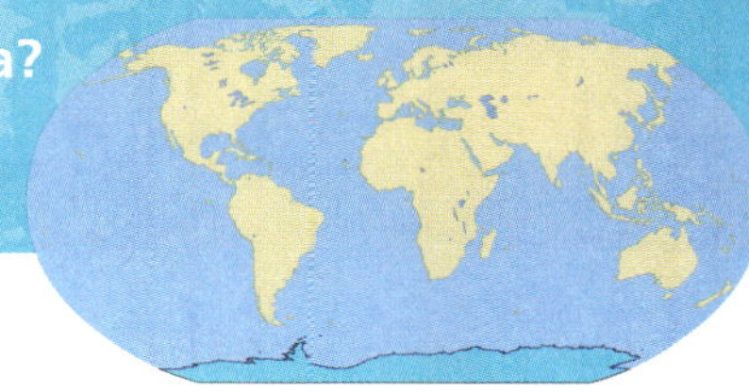

Lowest Recorded Temperature on Each Continent

Antarctica is the coldest place in the world.

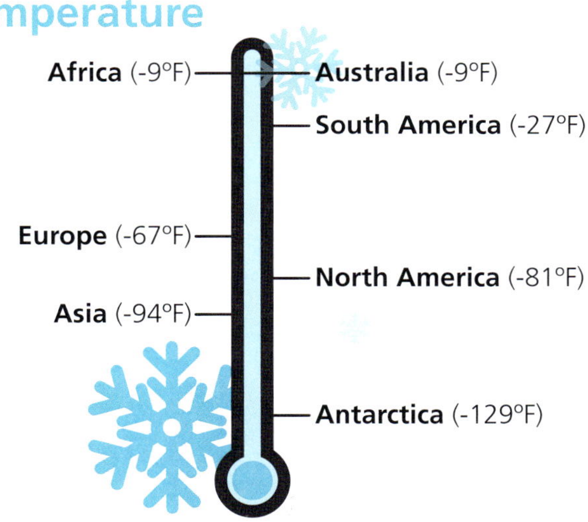

Did You Know?

The highest temperature ever recorded in Antarctica is 59° F.

Emperor penguins

Emperor penguins live in large colonies on the sea ice along Antarctica's coast.

Antarctic iceberg

As temperatures get warmer in summer, pieces break off Antarctica's ice shelves. The pieces can form huge icebergs.

Scientists in Antarctica

Scientists study Antarctica during the summer. Very few people stay on this cold, barren continent during the winter.

Antarctica through History

1700 — 1800 — 1900 — 2000

About 200 years ago
Explorers first sighted Antarctica.

About 100 years ago
A Norwegian explorer reached the South Pole.

About 50 years ago
Twelve countries agreed to use Antarctica only for scientific research.

Handbook of Map Skills

Geographical Terms

This drawing shows many features of the earth. To find the meanings of some of the terms, look in the word list below.

Canyon: A deep, narrow valley with high, steep sides

Cape: A narrow piece of land that extends into the sea

Coast: Land along a large lake, sea, or ocean

Desert: A large land area that receives little rainfall

Forest: A large land area covered with trees

Gulf: A large area of water within a curved coastline; a gulf is larger than a bay and smaller than a sea

Harbor: A protected body of water where ships can anchor safely

Hill: A small land area higher than the land around it

Island: A piece of land surrounded by water

Lake: An inland body of water

Mountain: Land that rises much higher than the land around it

Peninsula: A piece of land nearly surrounded by water

Plain: A large, flat land area

Plateau: A large, high land area that is generally flat

River: A body of fresh water that flows from higher to lower land

Sea: A large body of salt water partly surrounded by land

Valley: The lower land between hills or mountains

Coast

Desert

Forest

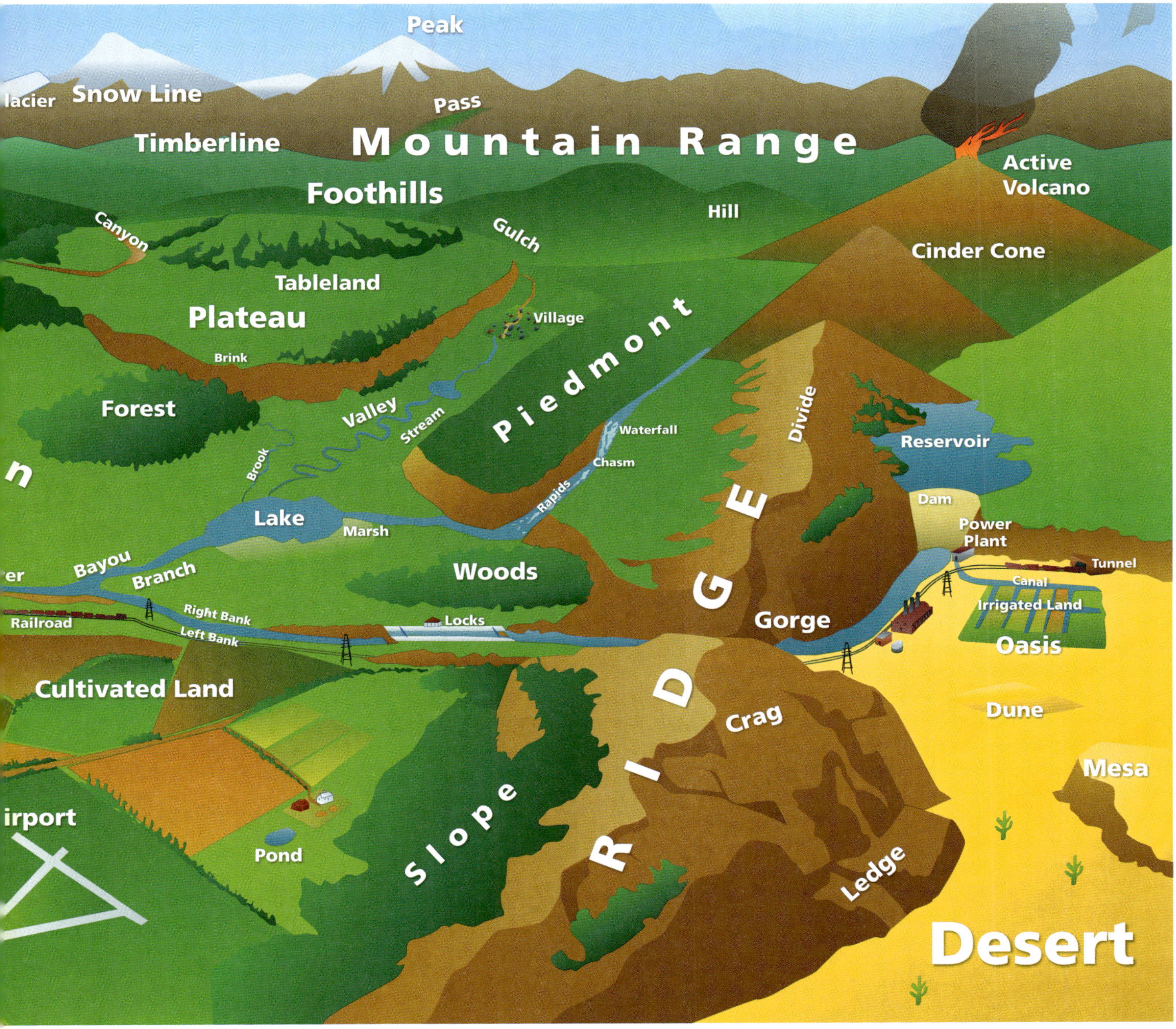

Harbor

Island

Mountain

Valley

Handbook of Map Skills

Map Question

What symbol on the map stands for a river?

Symbols

Symbols are lines, colors, and shapes that stand for something else. Maps use symbols to stand for real places on the earth.

Ocean

River

City

Mountains

Legend

A **map legend** explains what the symbols on a map mean.

South America	
(red line)	Country boundary
(blue line)	River
▲	Highest point
Bolivia	Country
⊛ Lima	Country capital
■ São Paulo	City
Atlantic Ocean	Ocean

Compass Rose

A **compass rose** shows directions on a map. The letters stand for **N**orth, **E**ast, **S**outh, and **W**est.

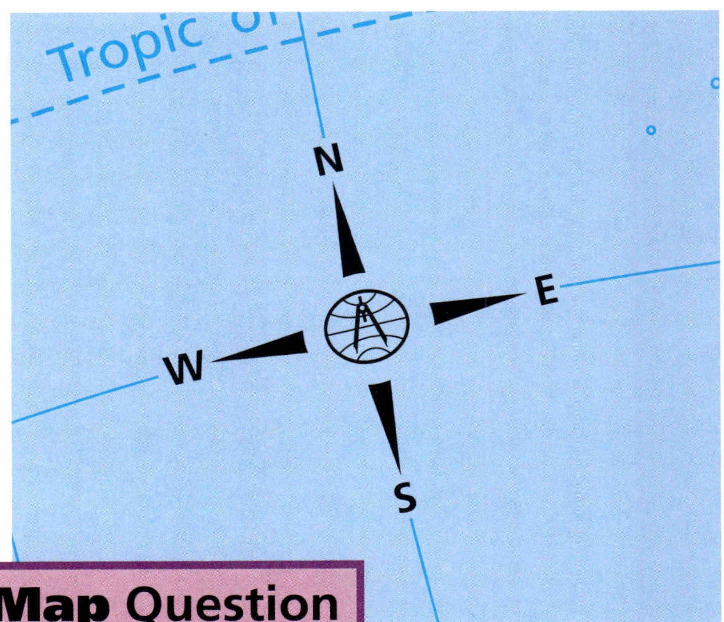

Map Question

If you are facing north, what direction is to the right?

Handbook of Map Skills

Bar Scale

A **bar scale** helps you understand distances on a map.

Place a ruler next to the bar scale on this map. You will see that one inch on the map is equal to a little more than 200 miles on the earth.

A bar scale helps you measure distances on a map.
Copy the bar scale onto a strip of paper.

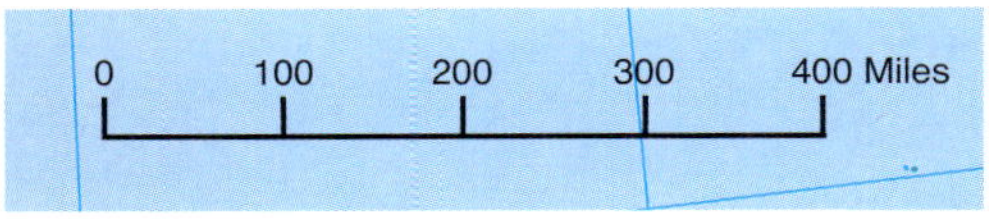

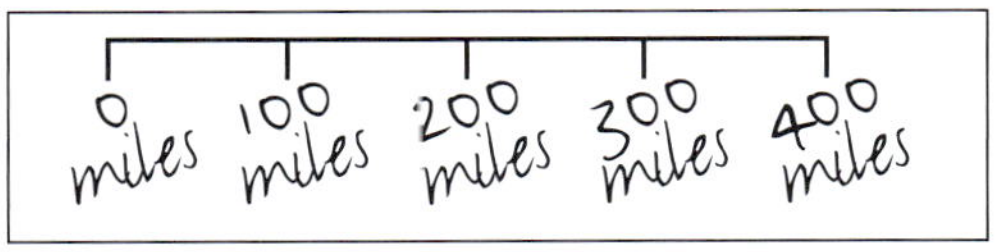

Use your paper bar scale to find distances on the map.

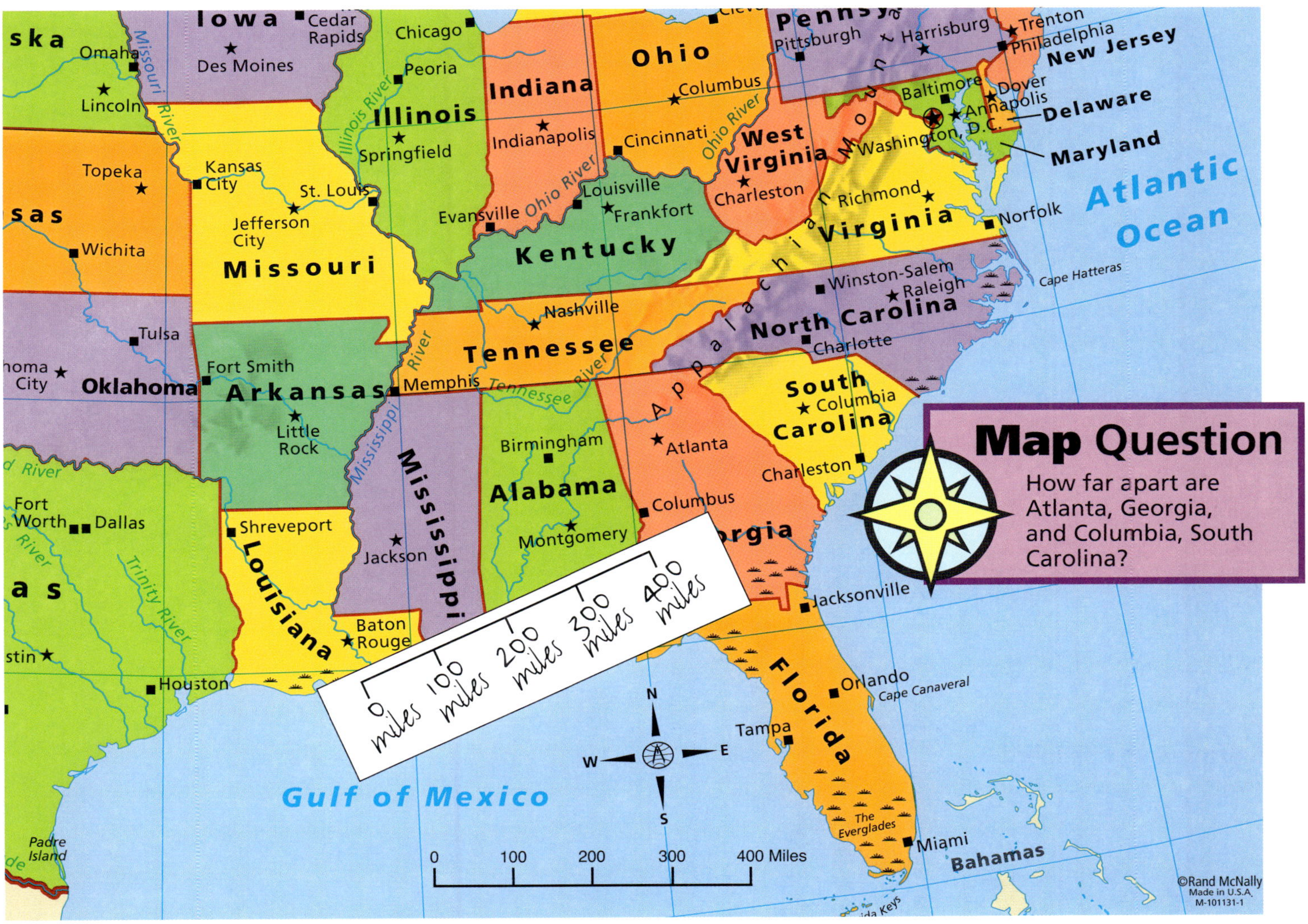

Map Question

How far apart are Atlanta, Georgia, and Columbia, South Carolina?

Baton Rouge, Louisiana, and Montgomery, Alabama, are a little more than 300 miles apart.

Handbook of Map Skills

Latitude

Latitude lines run east and west on globes and maps.

The **Equator** is a latitude line that divides the earth in half. It represents 0 degrees latitude.

All other latitude lines are numbered based upon their distance from the equator.

Each half of the earth is call a **hemisphere**.

All land and water north of the Equator is in the **Northern Hemisphere**.

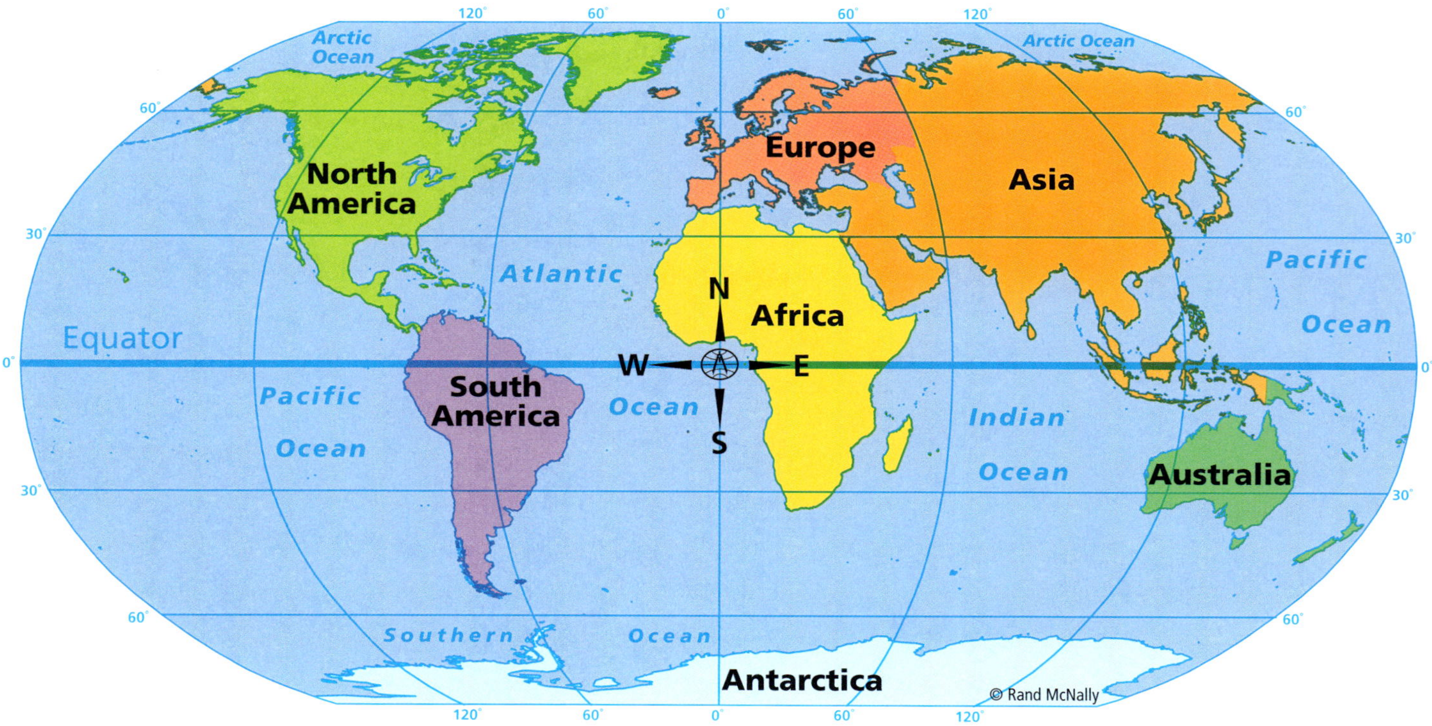

All land and water south of the Equator is in the **Southern Hemisphere**.

Longitude

Longitude lines run north and south from pole to pole on globes and maps.

The **Prime Meridian** is the longitude line that represents 0 degrees of longitude.

All other longitude lines are numbered based upon their distance from the Prime Meridian.

Each half of the earth is called a **hemisphere**.

All land and water west of the Prime Meridian is in the **Western Hemisphere**.

All land and water east of the Prime Meridian is in the **Eastern Hemisphere**.

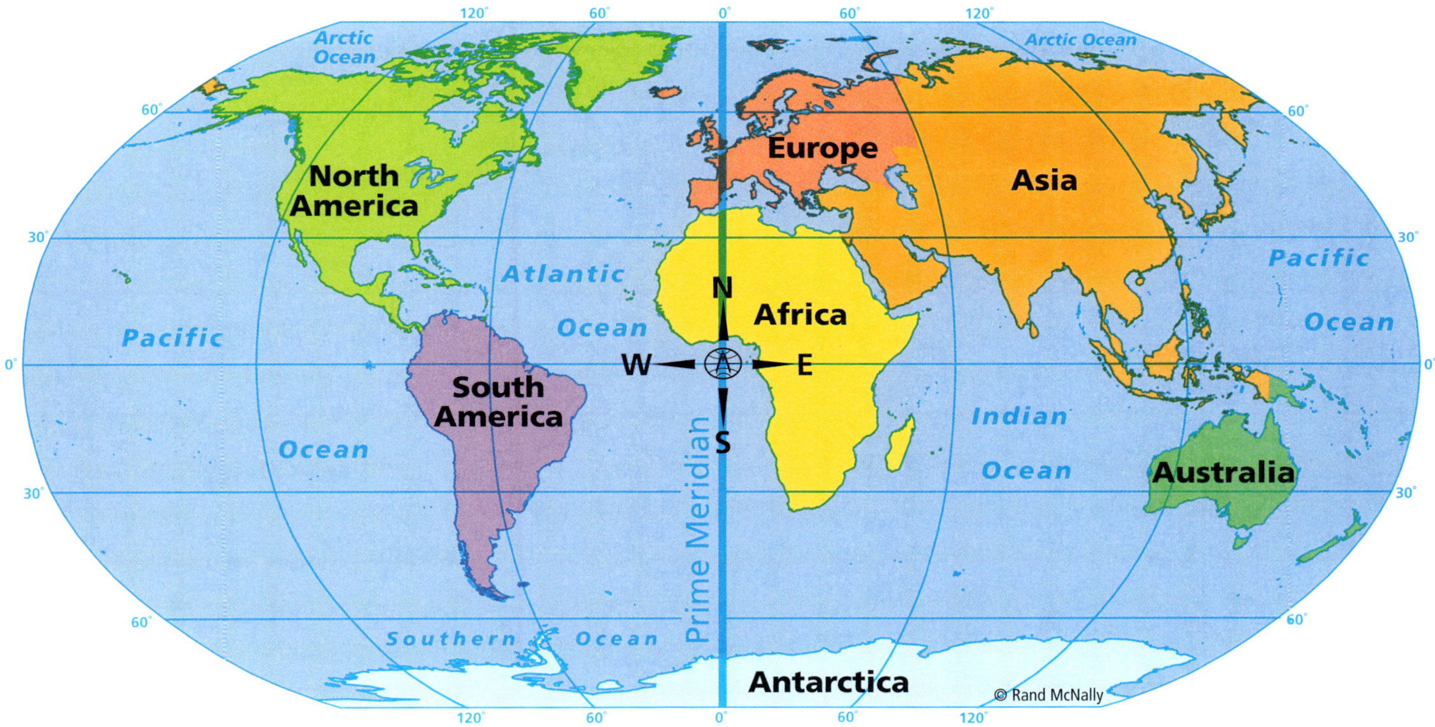

Map Question

In which two hemispheres is North America located?

Glossary

bar scale	the part of a map that helps you measure distances; the bar scale tells how many miles on the earth's surface are shown by each inch on the map
climate	how hot or cold, wet or dry a place is over a long period of time
compass rose	the part of a map that shows directions; the letters on a compass rose stand for North, East, South, and West
continent	one of the seven largest bodies of land on the earth
country	a land that has a government
country boundary	a line on a map that shows where a country begins and ends
Eastern Hemisphere	all land and water on the earth east of the Prime Meridian
Equator	the latitude line that divides the earth into the Northern Hemisphere and the Southern Hemisphere
globe	a model of the earth
hemisphere	half of the earth
latitude lines	lines that run east and west on a globe or a map
longitude lines	lines that run north and south on a globe or a map
manufacturing	making goods

map legend	the part of a map that explains what the symbols on the map mean
map	a drawing of the earth's surface
national capital	a city where a nation's government leaders work
Northern Hemisphere	all land and water on the earth north of the Equator
ocean	one of the five largest bodies of salt water on the earth
Prime Meridian	the longitude line that divides the earth into the Eastern Hemisphere and the Western Hemisphere
regions	places that have something in common
Southern Hemisphere	all land and water on the earth south of the Equator
sphere	a ball; the earth is shaped like a sphere
state	part of a country; the United States is a country with fifty states
state boundary	a line on a map that shows where a state begins and ends
state capital	a city where state government leaders work
symbols	lines, colors, and shapes that stand for something else
Western Hemisphere	all land and water on the earth west of the Prime Meridian

Index

Index Abbreviations

Afr. ....Africa
cap............... .....capital
Dem. Rep. ....Democratic Republic
D.C.....................District of Columbia
Eur.....................Europe
N.A. ....North America
S.A. ....South America
U.K.....................United Kingdom
U.S. ....United States

Index